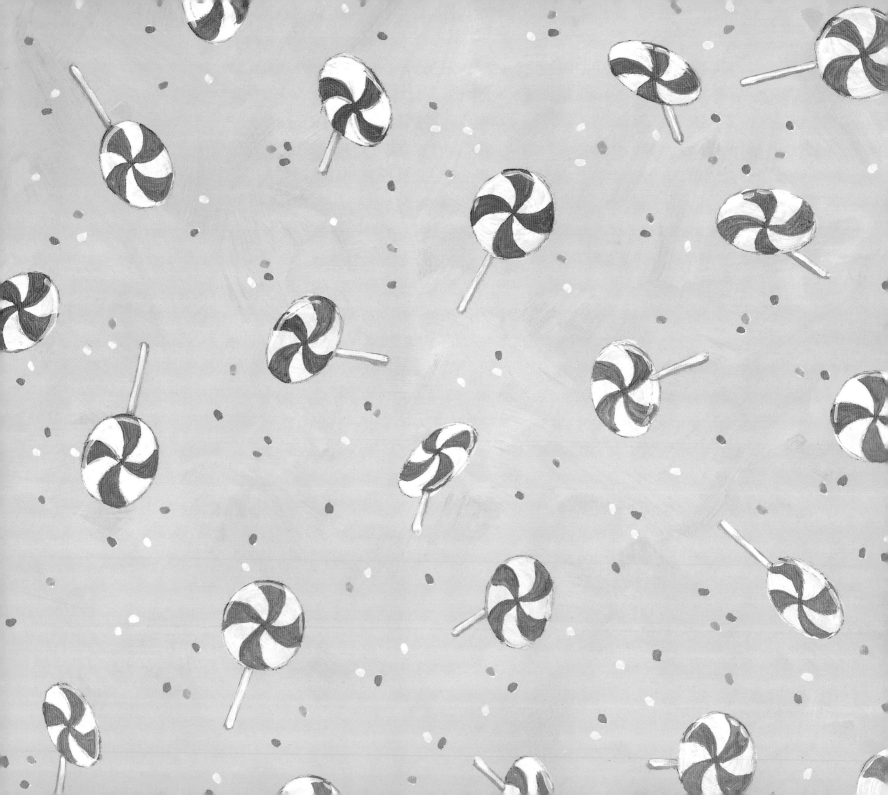

The Big Rock Candy Mountain

MONDO

For information contact:
MONDO Publishing
980 Avenue of the Americas
New York, NY 10018

Visit our web site at http://www.mondopub.com

Printed in China

04 05 06 07 08 09   9 8 7 6 5 4 3 2 1

ISBN 1-59336-062-2 (HC) ISBN 1-59336-063-0 (PB)

Edited by Susan DerKazarian
Designed by Annette Cyr

Library of Congress Cataloging-in-Publication Data

The Big Rock Candy Mountain / illustrated by John Kanzler.
     p. cm.
     Summary: Pa, Ma, and their children take a trip to the Big Rock Candy Mountain, with
its lollipop trees, chocolate fountains, and friendly bears wearing crazy socks.
     ISBN 1-59336-062-2 (hc) -- ISBN 1-59336-063-0 (pbk.)
     1. Children's songs--United States--Texts. [1. Voyages and travels--Songs and music. 2
Humorous songs. 3. Songs.] I. Kanzler, John, ill.

PZ8.3.B4837 2004
782.42--dc22
[E]
                                                                    2003056157

The Big Rock Candy Mountain

Illustrated by John Kanzler

MONDO

One evening as the sun went down

And the supper Ma was burnin',

Down the stairs came dear ole Pa,

And he said, "Kids, I'm not turnin'.

4

"I'm headed for a land that's far away,

Beside the chocolate fountain.

So come with me and we'll go and see

The Big Rock Candy Mountain."

5

Oh, the buzzing of the bees in the lollipop trees,

By the chocolate milkshake fountain,

Near the lemonade springs where the bluebird sings,

On the Big Rock Candy Mountain.

On the Big Rock Candy Mountain

There's a land that's fair and bright—

Where the jellybeans grow on bushes,

And you sleep out ev'ry night;

Where the hillsides are all grassy,

And the sun shines ev'ry day.

Oh, I'm bound to go where there's fresh white snow,

Where the rain don't fall and the wind don't blow,

On the Big Rock Candy Mountain.

Oh, the buzzing of the bees in the lollipop trees,

By the chocolate milkshake fountain,

Near the lemonade springs where the bluebird sings,

On the Big Rock Candy Mountain.

On the Big Rock Candy Mountain
The bears wear crazy socks.
And little streams of root beer float
Come tricklin' down the rocks.

Oh, the grown-ups all wear silly hats

And the teachers always grin.

There's a lake there, too, of marshmallow goo,

And you can paddle all around it in a big canoe,

On the Big Rock Candy Mountain.

13

Oh, the buzzing of the bees in the lollipop trees,

By the chocolate milkshake fountain,

Near the lemonade springs where the bluebird sings,

On the Big Rock Candy Mountain.

On the Big Rock Candy Mountain
The chairs have peppermint legs.
The big dogs all have rubber teeth
And the hens lay chocolate eggs.

The candy trees are full of treats
And the barns are full of s'mores.
Oh, I'm bound to go where there's fresh white snow,
Where the rain don't fall and the wind don't blow,
On the Big Rock Candy Mountain.

Oh, the buzzing of the bees in the lollipop trees,
By the chocolate milkshake fountain,
Near the lemonade springs where the bluebird sings,
On the Big Rock Candy Mountain.

On the Big Rock Candy Mountain
They dig for chocolate gold.
And if the truth is to be told,
You'll never catch a cold.

There's no such thing as salty tears,

No bruises, bumps, nor scrapes.

Oh, I'm bound to stay where you play all day,

Where the skies are blue and never turn gray,

On the Big Rock Candy Mountain.

21

Oh, the buzzing of the bees

in the lollipop trees,

By the chocolate milkshake fountain,

Near the lemonade springs

where the bluebird sings,

22

On the Big Rock Candy Mountain.

I'll see you all this coming fall,

On the Big Rock Candy Mountain!

The Big Rock Candy Mountain

Arrangement by Kathy Boyd and Mark Gensman

One eve-ning as the sun went down and the sup-per Ma was burn-in', down the stairs came dear

ole Pa, and he said, "Kids, I'm not turn-in'. I'm head-ed for a land that's far a-way, be-

side the choc'-late foun-tain. So come with me and we'll go and see the Big Rock Can-dy

Moun-tain." Oh, the buz-zing of the be-es in the lol-li-pop trees, by the

choc'-late milk shake foun-tain, near the le-mon-ade springs where the blue-bird sings on the Big Rock Can-dy

Moun-tain. On the Big Rock Can-dy Moun-tain there's a land that's fair and

bri-ght. Where the jel-ly beans grow on bu-shes, and you sleep out ev'-ry ni-ght.- Where the

hill-sides are all gras-sy and the sun shines ev'-ry day-ay. Oh, I'm bound to go where there's

fresh white snow, where the rain don't fall and the wind don't blow, on the Big Rock Can-dy Moun-tain.

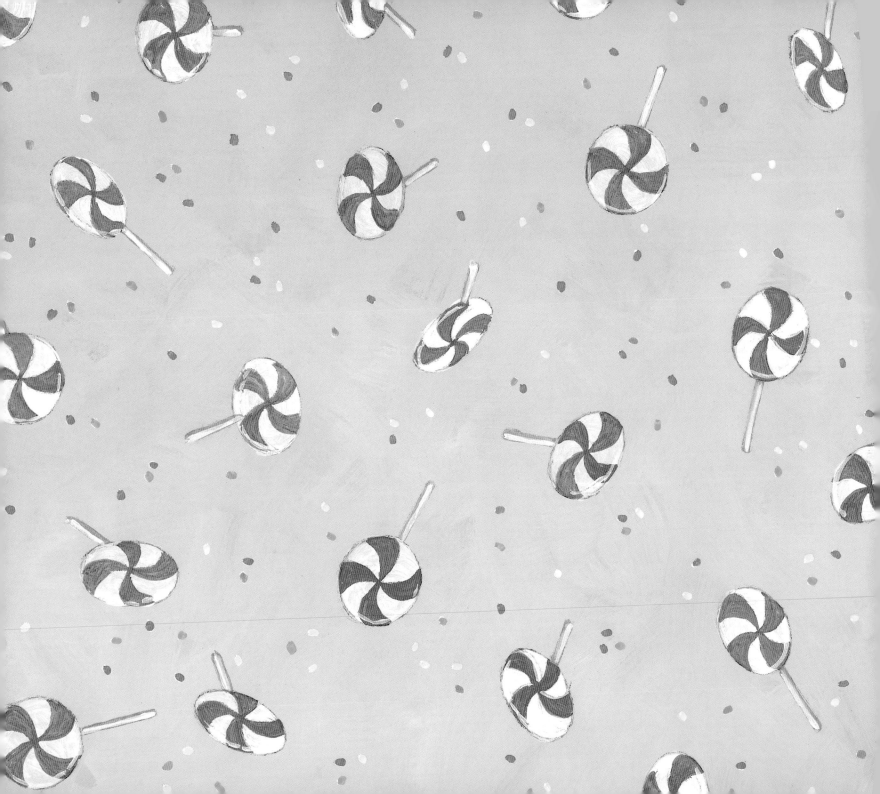

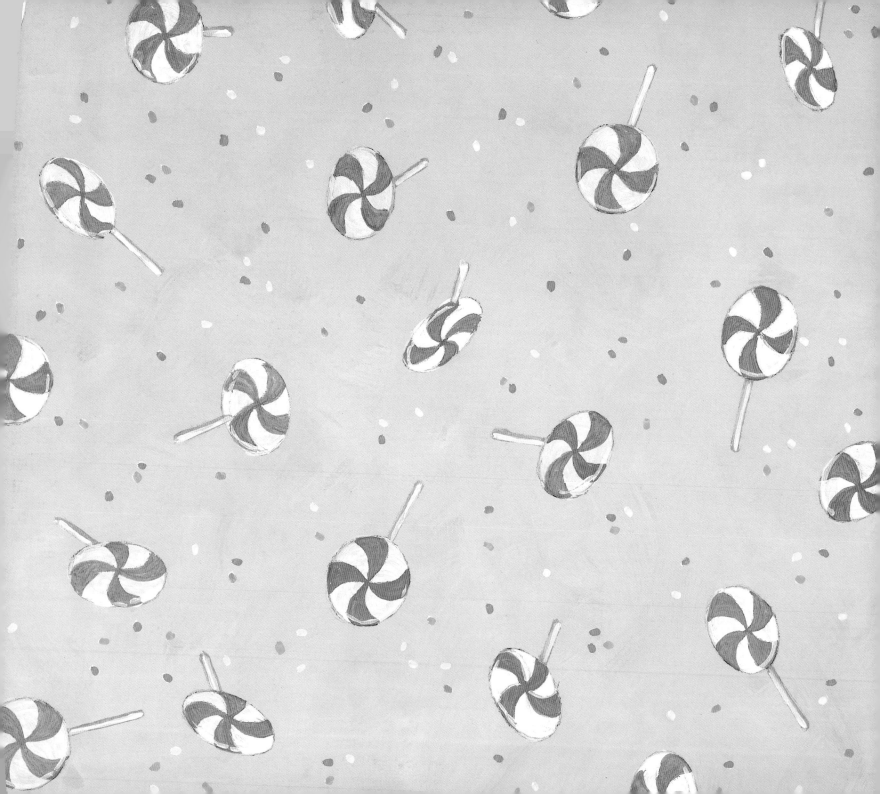